Eclipse of Tides

ALSO BY NGOZI OLIVIA OSUOHA

The Transformation Train
Letter to My Unborn
Sensation
Tropical Escape (with Amos O. Ojwang')
Fruits from the Poetry Planet
Poetic Grenade
Whispers of the Biafran Skeleton
Chains
Raindrops
Freeborn

Eclipse of Tides

poems by
Ngozi Olivia Osuoha

Poetic Justice Books
Port St. Lucie, Florida

©2019 Ngozi Olivia Osuoha

book design and layout: SpiNDec, Port Saint Lucie, FL
cover design: Kris Haggblom
cover image: *Mediterranean Sea*, 1857; Gustave le Gray

All rights reserved.

No part of this book may be used or reproduced in any manner whatsoever without written permission except in the case of brief quotations embodied in critical articles and reviews. Members of educational institutions and organizations wishing to photocopy any of the work for classroom use, or authors, artists and publishers who would like to obtain permission for any material in the work, should contact the publisher.

Printed in the United States of America.
Published by Poetic Justice Books
Port Saint Lucie, Florida
www.poeticjusticebooks.com

ISBN: 978-1-950433-23-0

FIRST EDITION
10 9 8 7 6 5 4 3 2 1

to my nephews and nieces
Lucky, Chioma, Emmanuel, Wisdom and Ihuoma

contents

My Pleasure	3
Intention	4
Unity	5
Power	6
Pollution	7
Ambition	8
Sacriledge	9
Victims	10
Fear	11
Suicide	12
Hate	13
Civilization	14
Be Careful	15
Pride	16
Ego	17
Self Esteem	18
Change	19
My Cloth	20
Society	21
Crime	22
Loneliness	23
Truth	24
Lust	25
Desire	26
Success	27
Politics	28
Failure	29
When I Am Angry	30
My Rose	31
The Dice	32

Naked	33
Pure	34
I Am a Writer	35
Africa	36
Heed	37
Never Do Wrong	38
Pushed	39
Murder	40
Election	41
Fame	42
Friends	43
Work	44
Coinage	45
The Piece of the Peace I Promised	47
A Piece of My Conscience	48
The Traveler	49
Wandering	51
The Mis That Mars	52
Hello Mr. Boss	55
Human Lefts	58
The Drunk Lawyer	59
The Guts of Nudity	60
The Pencil of God	61
Freestyle	62
Worries of a Migrant's Mother	65
My Window	70
acknowledgement	73
about the author	75

Eclipse of Tides

MY PLEASURE

When I close my eyes
I see you
When I open my eyes
I see you,
When I listen deep
I hear you
When I watch closely
You are everywhere.

You are my pleasure
The pleasure I breathe
You are my pleasure
The one I cannot measure
You are my pleasure
The bulk of my happiness.

I write for you
I sing or you
I live for you
I wait on you
I long to be with you

You're real, the most real
You are love, the fine love.

Ngozi Olivia Osuoha

INTENTION

Lo, watch it
For it could build
It could tear
It could grow
It would kill
Lo, guard it
Let it be courteous
True, tested and tried.

Lo, see it
See that it is real
See that it is just,
It is divine
See that it is favourable.

Lo, intention
It is a device
That could put on reverse
It is a measure
That could bring displeasure

Lo, intentions
They are hidden, hidden for missions.

UNITY

We need unity
To fight woes against mankind
We need unity
To subdue the earth.

Unity is the key
To face hunger and thirst
Unity is the key
To stop war and crime.

Unity is the map
To locate unemployment
Unity is the road
To get peace and harmony.

We need unity
Let us unite
For the world cannot survive
If we bomb, kill and murder.

Hey, dear unity
Come, come close
We bid you come,
We need you now and forever

Ngozi Olivia Osuoha

POWER

We have seen power
In the name of power,
We have seen power
Greed, malice and pain
All for power and power.

But still need power
Because it can heal and cure
We need true power
The one that will lead and guide.

So let this power be safe
That we all would be safe,
Let this power be peaceful
For our world to be peaceful.

Power should not be harmful
Rather tolerant and mindful
Power should not be fearful
Rather vigilant and careful

Let this power bind us
Let it not bleed us.

POLLUTION

They pollute, they pollute
They suffocate, they suffocate
They barricade, they barricade
They mount roadblock and blockade.

They pollute, they poison
They instigate, they incite
They puncture, they rupture
They contaminate, they infiltrate.

Yes, they pollute
They strangle in the jungle
They refill themselves
They cheer to merry.

They pollute, they pollute
Pollution beyond solution,
They pollute, they salute
Salutation beyond pollution.

This pollution is targeted
Calculated and propagated,
For reasons obvious yet unknown.

Ngozi Olivia Osuoha

AMBITION

The longing of a soul
 To take full control
The desiring of a heart
To be full on the chart
The yearning of a spirit
Never to have a limit
The ambition of man
To drive his own van.

Ambition, the great drive
The thing that ignites strive
Ambition, the railway
Hold on, lest you derail
Move on, lest you fail
Ambition, the point of life.

Cook it, boil it, and eat it
Live it, never leave it
Clean it, wash it, and build it
For your ambition is you
Let the world stand up for it.

SACRILEGE

It is amazing
And heartbreaking,
It is humiliating
And dumbfounding
How sacrilege finds its way.

Sacrilege, sacrilege
A bit of evil
A piece from the devil
Hunting men
Haunting human
Daunting humanity.

In the north
In the south,
In the east
In the west,
Sacrilege advances,
Penetrating, permeating
Advancing, raging
In strength, in energy
In anger, in full force,
Sacrilege, overtaking men.

Ngozi Olivia Osuoha

VICTIMS

The world is a plain
It flies our plane,
The world is a train
It moves our trend,
We are all here
We are all there,
Flying, moving and going
Victims, victims, we are.

A victim today, a victor tomorrow
A victor today, a victim tomorrow
Victims, victims, we all are
Victims, victims, we are all.

Lift the victims, love the victim
Save the victim, heal the victim
You are a victim, I am a victim
They are victims, we are victims.
Victims of society, victims unlucky
Victims of circumstances, victims unlucky
Victims of hate, victims of abuse
Victims of fate, victims of life
Victims of race, victims of religion
Victims of ignorance, victims, victims.

FEAR

I am afraid
You are afraid
We are afraid

I am frightened
You are frightened
We are frightened

I am fearful
You are fearful
We are fearful.

Fear is my enemy
Fear is your enemy
I am scared
You are scared
We are scared.

It is my foe
It is your foe,
It our foe.

We must live
We must fight
We must win.

Come, let us move
Let us win this fear
For fear is a beast.

Ngozi Olivia Osuoha

SUICIDE

It is a coward
It has no strength
It is awkward
It has no length.

Come, let us fight
We can win it
For it is not strong
Only a little while
We need be victorious.

Don't give in
Never mind,
Just a little while
The smoke shall clear.

Look away from pain
It does not last,
Look away from agony
Look upon the future
It is as beautiful as the rainbow
Look, the land is green.

HATE

When we hate
We kill,
When we hate
We abuse,
When we hate
We dehumanize
When we hate
We violate.

When we hate
We humiliate
When we hate
We exploit
When we hate
We persecute
When we hate
We bind.

Hate is evil
It does nothing good
Hate is unkind
It does nothing kind,
Hate is unfair
It does nothing fair.

Ngozi Olivia Osuoha

CIVILIZATION

You have come
To build us up,
You have come
To open our eyes.

You have come
To enlighten our path
You have come
To straighten our road.

Civilization, you are here
Yes, here to probe
To announce, to portray
To soften, to quicken
To hold and to bless.

Civilization, you have come
Yes, you have
Here to thwart, to distort
And to disturb,
Civilization, you are here
But a mystery,
A hidden agenda, one
Unfolding with time.

BE CAREFUL

Wherever you are
Wherever you go
Wherever you live
Wherever you work
Please be careful.

In a strange land
In a new place,
In an old home
In a fake abode
Anywhere you are
Be careful, be careful.

Strangers can win
Indigenes can lose
Visitors may live
Associates could prank
Be careful, be careful.

Ngozi Olivia Osuoha

PRIDE

Look before you leap
Sit before you lean
Plant before you harvest
Watch and pray
For pride goes before a fall.

Pride is a deadly weapon
It conceals fault
And explodes publicly
Then shaming the person.

Pride too is a virtue
It could be positive,
When properly managed
It becomes an attribute
Pride is good too.

But unnecessary pride ruins
It dooms too,
Pride is like a bomb
It could kill thousands
And bury millions,
Pride is a fantastic fallacy.

EGO

Ego, you are high
High like the mountain
Ego, you are up
Up there in the sky.

Ego, you are pompous
Pompous, even without need
Ego, you are arrogant
Arrogant without base.

Ego, you are rude
Rude, with no strength
Ego, you are faulty
Faulty, in the face of danger.

Ego, advice yourself
Learn from the past
Bend for the present
Calm down for the future.

Ego, watch your head
Cut your tail
Dust yourself
For tomorrow is a mystery.

Ngozi Olivia Osuoha

SELF ESTEEM

Build yourself well
Wear your shoes
Tighten your belt
And take a walk.

Fear no one
Let nothing trouble you
Fear no giant
Let no man intimidate you
You are a star
You are a giant too
A legend in the making.

You are worth it
Let no man tell you otherwise
You are great
Never feel belittled,
High up, high up, high up
Your self-esteem counts
High up, high up, high up,
Let nothing down you.

CHANGE

Wait for it always
In the morning
In the afternoon
In the evening
In the night
Change must come.

Wait for it always
From the positive,
To the negative
From the negative
To the positive,
It must come.

It can never always be neutral
For life evolves and revolves,
Life absorbs and dissolves
Wait for it always
Change must come.

To the left, to the right
From the right, from the left
Up, down, to and fro
Change constantly knocks.

Ngozi Olivia Osuoha

MY CLOTH

I am not beautiful
If only my cloth is,
I am not ugly
If only my cloth is.

I am not great
If only my cloth is,
I am not dazzling
If only my cloth is.

I am not shining
If only my cloth is,
I am not glittering
If only my cloth is.

My cloth is not me
My dress is never me
My make-up no matter how loud
My frame, no matter how weak
None can ever be me.

I am neither rich nor poor
If only my cloth is,
For my cloth cannot be me.

SOCIETY

Dear society
Every day, I weep for you
I pray openly and secretly
I call upon God to come
To come to your aid.

Dear society
I am tired and tired
You scare me to pieces
And frighten me to the marrows,
I weep and think and think
I ponder and ponder and ponder
I wonder and wonder and wonder
Because I see things beyond me.

Dear society
You have really gone far
I doubt your chances
I contemplate your advances
I recall your past
I cannot comprehend the present
For your future baffles me.

Ngozi Olivia Osuoha

CRIME

I hear of crimes
And doubt their reasons,
I hear of atrocities
And question their reasons,
Many a time, I pause
I meditate on the world
I ask myself several questions
And arrive at no answers.

Crime has become laws
Crime has become rules
Crime has become motto
Crime has turned flags,
It has become pledges
And coats of arm
Then I weep and weep for the land.

Crime, is fast raging
Sweeping across the world
Starving holy places
Desecrating altars
Abusing sacraments
And puncturing covenants.

LONELINESS

It can kill
It can murder
It can squander
It can ruin
Loneliness, a can of worms.

It has no friend
It has no foe,
It has no mother
It has no father
It has no brother
It has no sister
No aunt, no uncle
No niece, no nephew
Loneliness, a can of worms.

A lonely giant is gone
A lonely king is crazy
A lonely servant is lazy
A lonely prince is dead
A lonely princess is mad
Lonely paradise is hell,
Loneliness, a can of worms.

Ngozi Olivia Osuoha

TRUTH

The shining sun
And the moonlight
Clear and crystal.

The rains and drops of rain
The moving cloud,
And the beautiful sky.

The rainbow and her colours
The stars and their lights
Truth, the unquenchable fire.

The lightning and thunder
The day and the noon,
The night and the darkness,
Nothing can ever hinder.

Hide it, bury it, seal it
Thwart it, burn it
Truth, a piece of peace
A piece of time
A line of life
A branch of God.

LUST

The whirlwind
The cold breeze
The hot wave
The hurricane
The earthquake
The landslide
The rage, the tempest.

Lust, a dark cave
A black light
Destructive and regrettable
Dangerous and cancerous
Deadly and shady
Lust, a long way to drowning.

Run, run, run away
Fly, fly, fly away
Love it real, live it real
Lose it, a loss
Gain it, a gain
Lust, nothing progressive.

Ngozi Olivia Osuoha

DESIRE

A piece of my heart
The pump and the bit
The blood and the life
My desire, solely.

I tell you the truth
The peace of my pride
The ball of my eye
The cap of my knee
The feather in my cap
My desire, solely.

The overall plea
And the general prayer,
The highest bid
And the costliest feat
My desire, solely.

My heart is real
My soul is complete
My spirit is strong
My desire, solely
Lord, grant me.

SUCCESS

It is like a wave
It can sweep one off,
It is like a wind
It can blow one off.

It is like a storm
It can throw one off balance
It is like a fire .
It can burn one.

Success is good
Especially a good success,
Success is bad
Especially a bad success.

Success when maintained
Remains successful,
Success when abused
Remains abused.

Success brings pride
It sows jealousy
Success brings enmity
It plants hate and anger.

Ngozi Olivia Osuoha

POLITICS

I am confused
At your raking,
I am bewildered
At your fight.

I cannot comprehend
Whatever your mission,
I cannot decipher
What be your vision.

I am overwhelmed
By your forces
I am alarmed
By your rages.

Politics, I mean you
You are so unfair
Unfair and bitter
You are so unkind
Unkind and battering.

FAILURE

When you fail
Try again,
You may win.

When you fail
Get up,
Keep trying.

Failing is normal
Quitting is not.

Failure can happen
Even at the point of success.

Try, until you succeed
Succeed until you no longer fail.

Try one more time
One more time may be successful.

Failure is a lesson
It teaches much to learn
Open wide your eyes
Breathe deep and move on
For near lies success.

Ngozi Olivia Osuoha

WHEN I AM ANGRY

When I am angry
I pray
When I am angry
I write.

When I am angry
I cry,
When I am angry
I sigh.

When I am angry
I weep,
When I am angry
I wail.

When I am angry
I hope,
When I am angry
I believe.

When I am angry
I doubt
When I angry
I wonder.

MY ROSE

I have a beautiful rose
I will give it to my love.

I have a wonderful rose
I will give it to my heartthrob.

I have a green rose
It is just for my darling.

I have a yellow rose
Only for my angel.

I have a blue rose
I will give to my king.

I have a purple rose
Only for my prince.

My rose is excellent
My rose is attractive,
I will give it to my love.

Ngozi Olivia Osuoha

THE DICE

The dice is to inflict lice
The head gives them bread,
The tail grants them bail.

The dice is just to slice
The head mourns the dead,
The tail rains them hail.

The dice is for the rice
The head remains in their stead,
The tail helps them sail.

The dice pays their price
The head they have read,
The tails save them from jail.

The dice is their choice
The head is what they spread,
The tail delivers their mail.

The dice crowns them nice
The head is all they made,
The tail cannot make them fail.

The dice is a vice
The head makes us frail,
The tail prunes our rail.

NAKED

Born naked
Into a naked world
With life and death so naked.

Loved to be loved
Bare to the root,
But you stripped my heart.

Stripped me of peace
Stripped me of rest,
Joy and unity,
The world stripped of peace.

Ngozi Olivia Osuoha

PURE

Pure and clean
My love is unstained.

Beautiful and white
Without a blame.

You perched on me
Instead of staying firm,
Trusting and relaxing
You stood one-sided.

Ready to fly away
Because you were not real.

I AM A WRITER

I am a writer
And a thinker,
I am a poet
With a target.

I love fame
And good name,
I want to be a celebrity
But not with nudity.

I am a writer
I want to be a hero
Even from zero,
I want to make an impact
And still be intact.

I want to be a fact
With less to subtract.

Ngozi Olivia Osuoha

AFRICA

I am Africa
You are Africa,
We have norms
No matter the storms,
We have values
And great virtues.

It is our task
To tear the mask,
Let that be the game
It will not be a shame,
Because our unborn
Would mount on this horn.

This culture of strangeness
This tradition of alienness
Would do us great harm
Despite the charm.

HEED

I may be an old school
But not a complete fool,
There is a need
Our land cannot feed,
But if we nurture this seed
It can be our creed.

The land is weird
And the unborn, wild
Let us build a citadel
Not a brothel
For uncountable talents
Even for those with no parents.

Open wide the gate
And hatch their fate,
A gifted panel
Is a discovery channel.

Fame could still have privacy
Creativity should not suffer piracy,
When we make money
Make it as sweet as honey,
Not a whitewash
Or brainwash.

If you are decent,
You need no dent.

Ngozi Olivia Osuoha

NEVER DO WRONG

Quiet and lonely
Dark and tempting,
Great urge
Strong press,
But do not.

Have a rethink
A second thought,
Payday is real.

Seems rosy
But for a while,
Consequences
Had I known,
Prevention, healing is saving,
Do not do wrong.

Return good for no evil
Return evil for no good,
You will excel
From the roots.

PUSHED

Pushed to the wall
God knows all,
Hope is lost
God knows all.

Behind your back
Beyond your guts,
Above your reach
Before your nose.

Ngozi Olivia Osuoha

MURDER

No longer a stranger
But an insider,
No more in hiding
But bold and audacious.

With authority in the open
Chasing his game,
With alacrity in broad day light
Heading for doom.

A dance of the gods
Displaying at the market square
A clash of powers.

Murder is the lord
The legend, the king
The ruler, the leader
The giver, the taker
The chief, the thief
The master, the servant.

ELECTION

I do not know anymore
Nor can I understand
The meaning of election.

I see violence
I see violation,
I see humiliation
I see exploitation,
I see desperation
I see bitterness
I see hate.

Killings, murders
Unfairness, unkindness
Bound, bondage
Election, a wonder.

Ngozi Olivia Osuoha

FAME

You can attain it
You can achieve it,
You can work it
You can work for it,
You can get it,
You can reach it
You can be rich from it

You can maintain it
You can abuse it,
You can handle it
You can quash it.

Fame, you can dream it
You can imagine it,
You can visualize it.

Fame, you can like it
You can dislike it,
You can love it
You can have it.
You can hate it.

You can see it
You can feel it,
You can read it, fame.

Fame, good, better, best
Bad, worse, worst
Big, small, tall, short.

Fame, a game

FRIENDS

A good friend is an angel
A bad friend is a demon.

A good friend is a father
A bad friend is a beast.

A good friend is a mother
A bad friend is a monster.

A good friend is a sister
A bad friend is an abyss.

A good friend is a brother
A bad friend is a gangster.

Look out, watch out
Go for the real friends,
Be a true friend.

Live it, show it
Give it, spend it
Friends are friends.

Ngozi Olivia Osuoha

WORK

Life is work
Work is life,
Find it, work it.

Home is work
Live it, work it
Be there always.

Work is work
Work it, earn it
Do not spare it.

Bond is work
Bond it, work it
Let it work the bond.

Life is blessed
Work is blessed
Blessed, you live it
Blessed, you work it
Blessed, you bless it.

COINAGE

Before the break
I must be fast
And take my breakfast
With my can
And a teen
I head to the canteen.

The rhythm and beat
Cannot make up for rice
So lady Beatrice
Will still use the coin
At this age
I wonder the coinage.

With the corn
And the beef
Together with corn beef
Anything can still be stiff
Even the neck
For an unexpected stiff neck.

If you are red
Without the cross
You can still join the red cross
If you are black
And not a sheep
You can still be a black sheep.

Being sent out
From the cast

Ngozi Olivia Osuoha

Makes you no outcast,
You can bear a cross
For a special breed
You may not cross breed.

If you have all
And are mighty
It makes you no almighty
Having a bin
Filled with dust
Makes you no dustbin.

THE PIECE OF THE PEACE I PROMISED

The piece of peace I promised
The line of thanks I reiterated
The words of appreciation I pledged
The acknowledgement I proposed
You know I will never forget.

We won it together
Your prayers severed it
Your support heightened it
Your wishes elevated it
How then would I forget?

For your love, thank you
For your admiration, thank you
For your gesture, thank you
We are in this boat together
One by one we shall conquer
Day by day, we shall deliver
Bravo my people
This is just the beginning
In this year of our lord.

Ngozi Olivia Osuoha

A PIECE TO MY CONSCIENCE

Honestly, I do wonder
What put us asunder
We were inseparable
And tightly compatible.

You cautioned when I strayed
You directed when I prayed
You spoke when I got lost
You whispered at all cost.

We were close friends
We managed the bends
We were too close
Like, the eyes and nose.

Suddenly you went cold
And I terribly, bold
Unanimously, you got far
And I broke the jar.

Why are our conscience
Killed by science,
Murdered by technology
Or buried by theology?

Return dear partner
Be again our gardener,
Weed this our heart
Begin, please begin.

THE TRAVELLER

In the foreign air
Innocent or guilty
Home, midst in wail
Cold and love, faulty
There he is in anguish
Here we languish.

In the street, she is naked
Lonely and promiscuous
Home, life is crooked
Dying like hibiscus
None to understand
Not even the husband.

Killed or hanged
Clubbed and stabbed
Lynched and strangled
Teeming number in prison
Wearing scarlet and crimson
In a foreign land, to die.

Abroad and across the shore
Onboard slavery and hate
Onboard terrorism and racism
Walking on land mine
Accepting all wrong for peace
Swallowing all threats for life.

Dirty jobs, stinking meals
Foiled certificates and degrees

Ngozi Olivia Osuoha

Expired papers and big risks
Funny cops and rugged laws
Anger and extrajudicial zeal
No one to keep right, the wrong.

Home is backward
Away is forward
I am Edward
I must go toward
Lest I bruise leeward
For being onward.

WANDERING

Hungry and thirsty, I watched
Lonely and bored, I sigh
Burnt homes, bombed schools
We are the very tools.

Walking down the road
Trekking with a heavy load
No shade but barricade
No flee as I flee.

Nothing but war
No friend except terror
Life, meaningless
Death, the bitterness.

Crashed and crushed
Wearied and tired
Angered and annoyed
Battered and shattered.

Home, sweet home
Warmth gone, love dead
Friendship betrayed
Wickedness, portrayed.

Wandering and wondering
Wondering and wandering
Pondering and murmuring
Murmuring and wandering.

Ngozi Olivia Osuoha

THE MIS THAT MARS

Whatever is your take
Make no mistake.

If you are on the lead
Be careful not to misled.

You can be the guide
So avoid any misguide.

Watch your conduct
And curtail misconduct.

If you are there to represent
Make sure not to misrepresent.

Whenever you calculate
Strive not to miscalculate.

When you appropriate
Never misappropriate.

Even if you are not fit
Never be a misfit.

When you build trust
Avoid any mistrust.

All you manage
May you never mismanage.

Eclipse of Tides

Whoever you treat
Be bold, never mistreat.

Whatever you practice
Lead, and do no malpractice.

For the things you handle
Guard, do not mishandle.

Watch well your deed
Let none be a misdeed.

Life is a package
Please do not mispackage.

Life is a quote
Do not misquote.

In every report
Never you misreport.

You can also plead
But do not misplead.

When you print
Do not misprint.

Life too, is a play
Wrong, if you misplay.

Ngozi Olivia Osuoha

When you rule
Do not misrule.

When you win a prize
Make it no misprize.

Someday, you will judge
Then never misjudge.

As you inform
Avoid to misinform.

You can do a fire
But run from misfire.

Whatever you file
Pray against a misfile.

HELLO MR BOSS

Hello, Mr. Boss
He is not blind
And she lags not behind
He is not stupid
And she not timid
He is not a coward
And she can move onward.

He always abandons his food
And she stretches to be good
He knows no midnight
And she keeps her face bright
He sees you before his family
And she fades like the lily
Mr. Boss, are you?

He goes beyond job description
And she, below doctor's prescription
You ride him like a horse
And hard labour makes her coarse
He always accepts everything
And she complains about nothing
Wait Mr. Boss, hang on.

He sees your loopholes
And she still stands like poles,
He knows your every weakness
Yet she opts for kindness,
He finds you are lazy
She is not type-crazy
Mr. Boss let me finish.

Ngozi Olivia Osuoha

When there is an opportunity
You stoop below integrity,
You help those outside
While suffering those, inside
You choose to bless touts
And never to help poor dropouts
Hello, Mr. Boss, are you listening.

You always send him to danger
And make her a stranger,
Because he is poor
And she, behind the door
You use him like rag
And change her like bag
Mr. Boss, where is your conscience?

You think they have no choice
And they can bring no rice,
You do it more than thrice
Because they are nice
Soon, there will be a price
You will pay twice, twice
Mr. Boss, change your ways.

Mr. Boss, you are not God
So make light your rod,
Misuse not their loyalty
Because of your royalty,
Power is not a pure kingdom
Privilege is not a pure freedom
Mr. Boss, life is funny.

Eclipse of Tides

No matter who is your servant
He is better than a sycophant
No matter the feast
It is for men not beast
There is no greater landslide
Then that fought by pride
Be careful, Boss

There is always a payday
There may also be a waylay,
How we boss our subordinates
As though we own all planets
It is ungodly of us
If we lose on others, focus
Mr. Boss, you are human.

Arrogance is a gravity
Ego is close to insanity,
Impatience can cause atrocity
Dominance breaches audacity
Distinct collapses dynasty
Dishonesty scrapes maturity
Mr. Boss, we live but once.

Tomorrow is a puzzle
Despite the power tussle,
Tomorrow is uncertain
Do not draw the curtain,
Tomorrow, one is enthroned
Then, someone is dethroned
Bye, Mr. Boss, you can be nicer.

Ngozi Olivia Osuoha

HUMAN LEFTS

Nature is stiff

With a raw belief
It gives no freedom

So let us apply wisdom
Then, we rise to stardom
And become very flexible.

There is nothing like gender
We could be transgender
Just to this, surrender
Then it would be suitable.

Across, is the lesbian
Around is the gay
She will be our guardian
And he enjoys his day
So disturb not the bisexual.

They taught you the right
Leaving behind the left
That was a theft
You have the might
To take up the flight
And make it too casual.

The next will be animals
They too are mammals
Either a transanimal
Soon, we shall legalize marrying them
Because life is about choice
And anything can be twice.

THE DRUNK LAWYER

If you have no fears
The walls have ears,
In law, crimes have names
Though played as games.

Some ladies are sacred
Because they are well bred,
This is a public domain
Be careful who you stain.

Not all can manage
Image abuse and damage,
A lot you will miss
If your family leaves the stage.

Being excitedly raw
Sometimes breaks the law,
If your place was paradise
Some people would think twice.

Take some clues
If a mess continues
You would lose a certain friend
Except you comprehend.

Ngozi Olivia Osuoha

THE GUTS OF NUDITY

As cultures fall and slip
Everyone ready to strip
Kisses far from the lip
Transferred down to the hip.

Eyebrows shameless and booking
Eye lashes long and choking
Red lips hot and smoking
Fingers, claws and hooking.

Breasts flapping and greeting
Beams mounting them to the Everest
Contours banging, and meeting
Columns to maintain their protest
Tattoos scattered and irritating
Crazy fashion from the west
Cosmetics scaring and disgusting
Yielded, it becomes a quest.

Nurturing remains latent
Moderate, old and ancient
Coloured, that is the paint
Rainbowed, the true saint

Drawn from the well of timidity
Drank from the cup of primitivity
I had wondered the guts of nudity
Strong wine in open sheds
Orgy defining beds
Gay, nudity weds.

THE PENCIL OF GOD

If you write a poem
Scarcity prose
Long letter
Short verse
Melodious song
Small comedy
Love play
Mystery book
Life dictionary
Bitter dictionary
Bitter script
Little page
Worded history
Lettered story
Yet a busy note
Described in a high pitch
By a funny frequency
For a sagacious display
Then I am your pencil
Because you alone are God.

Ngozi Olivia Osuoha

FREESTYLE

We plead for your grace
To avert every disgrace
We seek for pure harmony
To dilute each disharmony
Give us our mantle
And may it never dismantle
Decorate our robe
And let none disrobe
Adorn our dress
And decode our address.

In life, as we press
May we never depress
In all the stress
Hear our call of distress
When you finally appear
May we not disappear
Then we shall be fine
As you alone define,
That makes us a member
And none can us, dismember

When we climb the rail
May we never derail
As you come to enthrone
May none, us dethrone
You shall keep our flower
And nobody can deflower
That gives us real accord
As you chase discord,
Then we shall impart
For no one to depart.

We must not promote
Anything you demote
What you import
We shall not deport,
All you compose
Nobody can decompose
You shall us, populate
And Satan cannot depopulate,
We shall be the virgin
For the bridegroom to disvirgin.

When we play our card
You shall not discard
When us, you revive
No trouble can deprive
Our peace will arrive
And we our joy derive
All these we must appreciate
For no gain to depreciate
Then we become an associate
Where nothing can dissociate.

Life looks sometimes similar
But actually dissimilar
So whatever we announce
Please do not denounce
Especially for atonement
Which helps our development
When we write a composition
Grant no decomposition
When we grow in population
Assign no depopulation.

Ngozi Olivia Osuoha

No matter the code
Someone can decode
It may not be a charge
So here in our base
May they never us, debase
Nor enter our place
Just us to displace
Rather may it remain our possession
With nothing like dispossession.

You none we trust
Despite our distrust
On you we notch
Please never us detach
You know our position
Make some disposition
However we join
Allow us not to disjoin
Then we shall possess
And not dispossess.

WORRIES OF A MIGRANT'S MOTHER

We sold all we had
So that he could travel,
We joined him to the airport
Intense prayers and warm hugs
Sweet kisses and hopeful goodbyes.

For some time, he has not called
Are you sure all is well?
My hypertension drugs have finished
The rheumatism has worsened
Even the arthritis.

He is not yet married
What could keep him so long?
The house he is building is halfway
His siblings' school fees unpaid
And his father is getting weaker.

My brilliant and intelligent son
Hopeful, green and young
My obedient and tamed boy
Lovely, careful and caring
Have my enemies succeeded?

I need my grandchildren
Those to sustain our lineage,
I need them while alive
Not when I am gone
Dear lord, where is my boy?

Ngozi Olivia Osuoha

The first time he came
He bought a new jeep
And shared money to people
Plumpy and chocolate
He looked hale and hearty.

Yes, beautiful like a woman
Braided hair, costly jewels
Soft, tender and smiling
Smelling good and fresh
Is that my boy?

Takes time to bathe
 Wastes time in the toilet,
Adjusting whenever I come around
A little naive and nasty
With coded words and languages.

My boy, my love, my pride
The son of my youth
The architect of my prime
The interpreter and interpretation of my dream
Where could you be?

I dreamt a boy was lynched
After being stabbed severally,
I saw he was helpless
Bled and bled to death
I hope it remains a dream.

Eclipse of Tides

They set him up with drugs
Late at downtown
Beat him with clubs and rods
Broke all his joints,
A different nightmare and dream

Hmmm, my girl, my angel
Committed and dedicated virgin
Loyal, submissive child
My pet, my everything
What is keeping you?

The last time you came
You looked hot and succulent
Breasts firm, big and erect
Buttocks hilly and mountainous
Hair, half shaved dread locked.

Always naked at home
In front of the computer
Only God understands that
Crazy phone calls, none stop
Nasty tones and suspicious.

Tattoos and weird makeup
You tell me they mean nothing
My angel, my colourful flower
We lived in a thatched house
Have ceiling, asbestos, decks destroyed you?

Ngozi Olivia Osuoha

I hear they sleep with dogs
Yes, I need grand children
Not poppy nor puppet
I hear they marry themselves
I got married to your father.

Yesterday at the farm
I saw a two headed snake
I ran home calling your name
Hoping you would answer
But you never did.

At noon, I saw the owl
Together with the vulture
They perched at the iroko tree
At the entrance was a millipede
All these are bad omens.

I dreamt a girl was tortured
Forcing a pole through her,
She was tied and hung
Helpless, voiceless, cryless
I saw too she died.

They lured her to the party
At the freezing side of the pool,
Did everything to her
Left her in the pool of her blood
Another frightening version of dream.

Eclipse of Tides

I woke up at midnight
The bed became a grave
The walls turned a ghost
The room chilled like a freezer
And the house almost a mortuary.

Your father turning and snoring
Sleeping like his last
I stepped out quietly
Into the thick dark night
Wondering about you.

Living is a problem
Dying is not the solution
Waiting may be in vain
Hoping may be futile
Where then are you?

I need no more money
I hate luxury and all
You are just my want
I need you right now
Please come home mamma's child.

Have they killed my son
Did they elope with my daughter
Has his friend turned his worst enemy
Has her lover killed her by abortion
Who saw my beloved child,
Mamma's wonder ?

Ngozi Olivia Osuoha

MY WINDOW

When I jump
I can land anywhere
When I run
I can reach somewhere,
But my window
Is not the route.

When I dance
I make you happy,
When I pray
I make you angry,
But when I sing
I carry you along.

My window
My door
My room
My roof,
My bed
My garden
My home
My house,
They all fold me close.

Eclipse of Tides

*Special thanks to
Godwin George
for helping to arrange the manuscript.*

about the author

Ngozi Olivia Osuoha is a Nigerian poet, writer and thinker. A graduate of Estate Management with experience in Banking and Broadcasting.

She has published ten poetry books and co-authored one (with Kenyan literary critic Amos O. Ojwang').

She has featured in more than forty international anthologies and also has published over two hundred and fifty poems and articles in over twenty countries.

Many of her poems have been translated and published into other languages, including Spanish, Romanian, Khloe, Farsi, and Arabic, among others.

She has won many awards; she is a one time *Best of the Net* nominee, and she has numerous words on marble.

www.ingramcontent.com/pod-product-compliance
Lightning Source LLC
Chambersburg PA
CBHW030102100526
44591CB00008B/230